il virus

Other books by Lillian Nećakov

The Lake Contains an Emergency Room, Apt. 9 Press, 2015
Hooligans, Mansfield Press (a Stuart Ross Book), 2011
The Bone Broker, Mansfield Press (a Stuart Ross Book), 2007
Hat Trick, Exile Editions, 1998
Polaroids, Coach House Books, 1997
Tiny Elvis, Suburban Home(made)Sick Press, 1995
Sickbed of Dogs, Wolsak and Wynn, 1989
Listen, Pink Dog Press, 1988
A Cowboy in Hamburg, Surrealist Poets Gardening Assoc., 1985
And Crunch, Proper Tales Press, 1982

il virus

Lillian Nećakov

An imprint of Anvil Press

"a feed dog book" for Anvil Press

Anvil Press Publishers Inc.
P.O. Box 3008, Station Terminal
Vancouver, BC V6B 3X5
www.anvilpress.com

Imprint editor: Stuart Ross
Cover design: Rayola.com
Interior design & typesetting: Stuart Ross
Author photo: Andrew Avalos
feed dog logo: Catrina Longmuir

Library and Archives Canada Cataloguing in Publication

Title: il virus / Lillian Nećakov.
Names: Nećakov, Lillian, 1960- author.
Description: Poems.
Identifiers: Canadiana 2021013271X | ISBN 9781772141733 (softcover)
Classification: LCC PS8577.E33 V57 2021 | DDC C811/.54—dc23

Printed and bound in Canada

Represented in Canada by Publishers Group Canada. Distributed in Canada
by Raincoast Books; in the U.S. by Small Press Distribution (SPD).

The publisher gratefully acknowledges the financial assistance of the Canada
Council for the Arts, the Canada Book Fund, and the Province of British
Columbia through the B.C. Arts Council and the
Book Publishing Tax Credit.

The Canada Council | Le Conseil des Arts
for the Arts | du Canada

BRITISH COLUMBIA
ARTS COUNCIL
An agency of the Province of British Columbia

Canada

for Aria and Miles

I

I woke to the sound of birds whispering about
the humans
and I couldn't tell any of you yet
because you were all
including the dog
sound asleep and the peace that filled the house
was like a giant breath
and the sun draped itself over every germ
and there was no need for anyone
to pray
even those of us who were awake
carrying the arrogance of stupid nations on our shoulders
as if a war was coming
as if no one would ever wake again.

2

The heart is happiest
when it hears its echo

that's been on the tip of my tongue for days now
a thing I couldn't quite put my finger on
the pulse of it

I remember now
we kept a suitcase by the door
the cows stood ever so still

afraid we might leave them
at the foot of the mountain
at the edge of the graveyard

I remember now
steam rising off the fields
one last breath before we began
counting life in dog years

before words were heavy as horses.

3

II a.m.:

dog seems frail as a wisp of smoke
husband turns 60

the sky strips
scars as gaping as the Chattahoochee

even if we called
the firefighters would not come

would not
wake this sleeping fire.

4

The voice of Etta James hangs
there, where the moon should have been
no, not like a eulogy
but a house filled
with continents of lost words
and the distant clanging of bells

well
we all gotta make a living.

5

The grocery list grows legs and leaves us
to stand with the trees
in silence
in shadow

the boxing gloves are off
winter's long hold loosened
soon the buds will flower into a thousand haiku
that no one will notice

then
we will cajole each other
out of our pyjamas
to meet the sun

laughing
tongues peppered with the seeds
of a new language
buckshot and breathless

ready for August, September
and so on.

6

Hand in hand in hand in hand
in hand
Williamsburg wedding
pigeons, carnations, a mouthful of air
later, maybe persimmons
and a wish to get
to heaven

Bourbon Street
launderette, chairs and lifeguards
music-dizzy, mouth to mouth
to mouth ecstasy
spring rain so much like
radiation
later, we will gather
to choose new saints.

7

After ten days of news, shouting, unbearable silence
we dust off the Grunow model 520
turn the dial in search of
Radio Luxembourg
yes
we *are* old enough to remember
yes
we *are* old enough to die

instead we huddle with the dog
that has been so puzzled by our movements
these last days
huddle
at 10 p.m. on a Saturday night
in wait of
At Two-O-Eight
dance music with the Russ Morgan Orchestra

only it's not 1956
and the train is coming faster than we think
and we have forgotten how to dance
and the knife sharpener, the one we thought
was an atheist
is crossing himself
we see it on the news
but it's 2020
and no cross

not the blue cross
not the red cross
not the holy cross
can save us
it's just another Saturday night

one for the books.

8

If my father were alive
he would forget each new day
that holding hands and walking
was forbidden
he would step out into the street
over and over
in search of crocuses
and I would hesitate
only for a moment
before pulling him back
into my embrace
again
for the last time.

9

In the dream that is not mine
a woman's face idles
at the bottom of the lake

the boys kneeling on the shore
just want to fish and they really should
button those coats

against the cruel days coming
yet they take off their shoes
roll up their pants and wade

the fish cave in
brush against frozen toes and hands
so much like seagrass

hats discarded in the reeds
fishing rods tangled in the blue maiden cane
a club of their own
under a moon rising like a hunter

already forgetting about ink-stained
rucksacks left dangling
somewhere
on childish coat hooks.

When we were six
tender acts of love:
small, soft, unbreakable
the family dog
the grace of someone's hand
the tooth fairy and air itself

when we were twenty
our hearts muscled through
lust and heartbreak
like revolutionaries
skin to skin
in the back seats of dark cinemas

when we were thirty
Gershwin and Buddha and Paz
loved us better than anyone had
at least that's what we thought
then
at thirty

when we were thirty-eight
the stretch of skin across a belly
full as a flood
a ferocious tide of heart swell
a catastrophic grasp of
each and every regret.

II

Remember 1977
when we ate lunch in the abandoned greenhouse
and there was a small hole in my dress
but you said
I love you
just the same

remember how we gathered all our thoughts
into a dark pile
resembling a magpie
left it there
for the gardener or the baron
whoever returned first

and remember too
how the machines all sounded
like they were reciting a sad poem
while we sat hostage
at the whim of philodendrons
orchids and
hydrangea.

12

Here we are again at the same
kitchen table
day 13
hostages dreaming of juniper berries
elsewhere rockets and bombs
in place of northern lights

garnet sky

Aria says we are
"doing WWII cooking"
I wish it were that simple
as I assume my yellow vest
walk out the door
and ask the dog to fetch.

13

In case we never meet
I forgive you

because
that's what people do

especially now that the zambonis
are silent as a body
stopped breathing.

14

The doctor's name reminds me of an opera
my son lives 850 metres away
may as well be a hallucination
we are running out of dish soap
I am afraid to kiss my husband
the world looks like a broken roller coaster
I haven't touched money in weeks
there may be funerals
I won't be able to attend.

15

There's a chair on the stage
folded clothes
a bird's nest
and a storm
a cop's voice singing
I miss you I miss you I miss

there's a minefield waiting out the door
if we're lucky
a Galway Saturday night down the road

there's a trash bag full of names
and a broken bicycle pump
at the curb.

16

Ron Padgett tells us
hope for everything

a knock at the back door
a bouquet of bluebells
shadows flocking together like geese

ah, the buoyancy of memory

Eliot told us
April is the cruellest month

I understand we have run out of ink
ransacked the pantry
the rain is like a sloppy kiss, the air tastes like chemo

yet a postcard arrives from Kingston

Galway Kinnell
burned in the wilderness

we long for roll call
the open mouth of a stranger, the prick of a sea urchin
the chesterfields of our childhood

and the clouds
continue their audition.

I tell them
I tell my children

holler past the fever house
holler
holler past god is not acting like god
holler past to calmer days
holler past lonely jugglers
juggling syphilitic typewriters
once typed, we did
holler past your very address
holler past you are stuck in this pig shit
4 a.m. skin on fire
holler
holler past tree and bush and leaf
holler past kill count
wings and manuscripts
mathematics of the edge
holler past the world is flat
holler past the krankhaus
the spielhaus
the bookhaus
holler past god dammit
holler past river you once
drowned in
holler
holler past the wild wild.

18

Pulse =
rapid fire
oh shit! my library books are late!

never
mind
the pool has been infected
we now have our own little Hiroshima

the year will pass like a glance
so too the explorers will come
and tip their hats
to those still standing.

19

Data from the seismometer at the observatory in Brussels:
the earth is speaking in tongues

if it were 1957:
we would be harvesting spaghetti in the Valley of Po.

Today we walk
and recite the rules
no dancing
no hopscotch
no stamp-licking
no whisper me to sleep

last night I cut my husband's hair
today we walk
past the missionary home
past the Order of the Holy Cross
where I once stopped on a frigid January night
to witness a small ceremony
I could not comprehend

today, while we walk
bp pops into memory
loose-jawed and shameless
in Nick's back garden on Tyrell Ave
all those years ago
skin crawling with life and laughter
unleashing his lexicon
like a prison break

today
you stand on the right
pass on the left
this is the choreography of life.

Home schooling
read from right to left, love
no, this is not maths
or Shakespeare
this is how the world ends

auuaaagguuuauaccuucccagguaacaaaccaaccaacuuucgaucucu
uguagaucuguucucuaaacgaacuuuaaaaucuguguggcugucacu
cggcugcaugcuuagugcacucacgcaguauaauuaauaacuaauuacu
gucguugacaggacacgaguaacucgucuaucuucugcaggcugcuuacg
guuucguccguguugcagccgaucaucagcacaucagguuucguccgggu
gugaccgaaagguaag

beginning of the genome sequence for multiple COVID strains.

22

There is graffiti in Alexanderplatz

on this side
stupid, stupid boys
light matches

watch the mountains panic.

Buzz Aldrin is sitting in my living room
he has a small bag
full of honeymoons
his handshake is lethal
he shows me the place on his arm
he once wished was graced
with a name tattooed in ruby red
I tell him
I am frightened
of
I don't know what
he stands, opens the window
letting in the eventide
the smell of rain
and an entire New Orleans jazz band.

24

Corazon,

at 3 p.m. there will be nerve food
to strengthen the heart
morph the grimace
wash away the gunpowder

at 5 p.m. the occupation might end
or we could just sit on the porch
reading Lorca.

25

Some of us are holding up the sky
with hockey sticks

as if it were a fairy tale
or a hall of fame

some of us are making a new republic
of letters

in dark rooms
while chewing off our fingers

some of us are returning to bar mitzvahs
in Vegas

over and over again
to feel the wail of history.

They're spilling milk by the truckload
and we're talkin' 'bout a pink moon rising
there's a man in Montgomery dying
to be an angel
and we're talkin' 'bout a pink moon rising
there's me and the thunder and the sky
a broken trinity
and we're talkin' 'bout a pink moon rising
there's a monk eating pretzels
over a letter board
and we're talkin' 'bout a pink moon rising
there's a house of cards filled
with an injured syntax
and we're talkin' 'bout a pink moon rising
there's a pile of leaves at the end of my lane
in the shape of a freakshow
and we're talkin' 'bout a pink moon rising
there's a recklessness growing inside us.

.

27

I have only one wing
no science can cure
the curve of my lung or
the fallen territories breeding
along my spine
still
it's blackberry winter
and we're all buying tickets
to someday.

28

How the fuck does my dog
know about Hieronymus Bosch

and how
can he transfigure the entire afternoon
into a tangerine gondola
brimming with dainty verbs.

29

The paper bag at the door
is filled with algebra
the reunion of broken parts

you were hoping
for lettuce and pears.

30

The department of dream corrections
is closed
something about
la resurrección

and so we continue
in wakefulness
sentence after sentence
stuck in our grammar box
among the wilting fruit.

31

After breakfast
we walked
then knelt in the daffodils
without explanation
like an unkempt junto.

Red-eyed jailbirds
are burying the dead
in a different potter's field
with trembling hands

each box marked with an X
in lieu of
sister
mother
son
hellion

no ablutions
no Sunday best
just a barge ferrying us
through Long Island Sound
one knot at a time
to Hart Island
where ghosts of the union army
spill the tubercularium blues.

33

The taxidermist's house
leans into the wind
all the days of April
we see it every
round the block
today I take my time
witness the frenzy
of letters strewn across
the porch
and for some reason
I think of the almost
horse-and-buggy days
when Gord
(This Ain't the Rosedale Library)
and I went to the Masonic Temple
to see the Pogues
then walked through
the hieroglyphics
of Bloor Street
all the way to High Park
and suddenly I understand
the architecture of my life
and I walk and I walk and I walk.

34

Here we go again
with the chopsticks
even though there is no
Thai takeout tonight
as if eating fried potatoes
with wooden sticks
will make us anonymous
as if being anonymous
will make them miss us
less.

Bloody Sunday
decades later
everyone's
either praying
or sharpening something

there's an army of suns here
while the Bogside
aches under the wreckage of rain

and the Derry girls wail
"Sunday bloody Sunday"

Rossville Flats rings
with bullets
washing flaps on the wind
in Glenfada Park courtyard

and the Derry girls wail
"Sunday bloody Sunday"

there is a trailer park
filled with a thousand
Boris Johnsons
hair like a cloud of terror
but don't worry, child
we're headed elsewhere.

Raymond Carver is a library
unweeded
overgrown and tangled
with democracy

he is a prince
a coward
a string of pearls
on the lips of a nation

his hands are soft
as a silk ribbon wrapped
around the budding
broken machines.

37

The myna birds are on furlough
Carl Reiner is singing
Nessun Dorma
over the airwaves
we are doing sit-ups
and playing donkey kong
some say we are lucky
but I think
we are just small fires
burning in the zone of alienation.

38

My mouth is lonely

I blow you a kiss
like heroin
while the fascist trapeze monkeys
aren't looking
then we are as cozy
as a school of Scarpace fish.

39

The dominoes declare themselves
sovereign
and refuse to play
the house too is tired
of the fact
of our bodies

we rummage through
the button jars
as if triaging

soon the day will be
bookended
by unmade beds
and wildly primped
hair

then, it will be
as you were.

40

From this day
forward
the mortician wishes
to be a giraffe

he will take his sassiness
out on the topographies
of the living
he will whistle Dixie.

41

Soon it will be
Memphis in June
only it won't

soon all the silence
we clung to
will ripen
into a volcano
filled with broken sternums

soon it will be
stranger days
only it won't.

42

The mercury is falling
like a Cooper 20 bomb

I'm thinking about
occupations of great cities
the Bosporus shivering
in the loneliness of morning
Christ as a peg-legged
wandering Jew
arms extending
over centuries
like an ancient magnolia

I'm thinking about the house
my mother died in
on Runnymede Road
of a broken cancer heart
the nurse I need to hug
but whose face I don't
recognize

and I'm thinking
about the brother
who fished me out
of the Adriatic
to flounder through
these days of valour.

43

The sandwich shops are closed
New York has put away its teeth

deserted fedoras flutter
across 5th Avenue

no more his girl Friday
belly laughs in the metro

everything is adagio
holding on to a minute ago

rock doves making love to
flinching sidewalks.

44

Feels like we're living
in a zoological garden

when
Doc Brown, PhD
cruises by in his DeLorean
stops to riffle through his trousers
pulling out a few billets
to the Pax Romana

we cheer and roar
possibility

hypothesis is one thing
mathematics is absolute.

45

Three cellos address no one
in the silence factory orchestra

there are no rules
on escalators ferrying ghosts

waterlogged oars
usurp the pond like unwanted lodgers

gasoline pumps
arrive at dangerous conclusions

I wait patiently like a fifth-grader
for the lesson to begin

my bones have limits.

46

The melting iceberg reveals
a tinderbox
and a Viking's beard

evanescing bergy bits baring
the circumference of
possibility.

47

There is weather
in Billings, Montana
the border is a cloud

medicine crow
high bird
over whistling water

yellowtail
warbling
the battle of bighorn

Sunday gone
great chief sleeps
under a cold kiss sky.

48

This afternoon we ate beans
we were suspicious of no one
the sun was a little drunk
and kept falling to its knees
a snippet of song
wafted through
our open window
like rice paper
a Saturday like so many others
heartening us
into the folds of future Saturdays.

49

Little Oyster island
settles into New York harbour
like a frail father
mudlarking for his radiant
sons
it begins raining
echoes
the fahrenheit wishes
it were celsius
and the gibbet tree
moves mountains
to silence it all.

Reading *Revolutionary Letters*
on the front steps
waiting for
the drag queens
Dudley Do-Right
Sir David Attenborough
Cripple Creek
Pinetop Perkins
Muddy Waters
Paul Butterfield
Bobby Charles
Ronnie Hawkins
the sky turns all
tubular bells
suddenly I am gripped
by fresh fear
and retreat
through the corridors
to a peace on the verge
of extinction.

The San Francisco Anti-Mask League
sends letter after letter
in the shape of a gun

we hide behind shuttered windows
drinking Manhattans
in jaunty yoga pants

down on Bay Street
a gaggle of dispossessed souls
grieve the tenderness of dawn.

Somewhere far from here
the sweet acacia trees
are in bloom

in Cape Town a statue
of Just Nuisance
the sailor dog who never went
to sea

at 59.3293° N, 18.0686° E
the Stockholm meteorological station
tracks and converts
our jolliness
into a Fellini film

the lint in my left pocket
is ∞ to the hours spent
moving from kitchen
to anguish
to puddle
to the evening
ovation.

53

The bluebells are distraught
over
the sun's false promise
the wind chill's cruel fold
and the hail
so much like wee bites
from seasons past.

54

On waking, I realize
the Anthropocene
along with the bread
is gone
in its place
a suspicious rendezvous
of mistral and malicious
cloud

and in the corner
the bottomland's
Eremocene.

55

Beneath the 49th parallel
the cruelty project
blows the house down
scrapes the skin off
the living
leaves language
voiceless

meanwhile
well-mannered Canada
goslings in mukluks
are rewarded with peace
prizes
under the flicker
of northern lights.

If I sewed my hands
finger to finger
could there still be
space enough
for shadows
would you watch
as the needle loitered
before moving through
bone and tendon

and if later
I removed the stiches
to run each finger
through your hair
would it feel different?

57

I am afraid I will forget
the Dewey decimal system
it's been weeks since
I've shushed teenage boys
and sat at my desk
in the little library
on St. Clair Ave

I am afraid
the books
won't understand why
they've been left
in the dark
and no one is
holding them

I am afraid that when
we return
an apology
will not be enough.

58

In the shock of spring
the earth dawns
black and blue
to greet its passengers

there will be no moorage
charge this or any other day
dream your dreams
writhe through
your nightmares
my codex is filled
with names of those
who love me most.

59

When suddenly halfway
through the afternoon
you recall dreaming about
Jackie Gleason
by your side on
a rollercoaster high
above Chauncey Street
next thing you know
you are on the *Cavalcade
of Stars* auditioning
for *The Honeymooners*
and it's 1951
the colour has bled
out of everything
and your hair is black
and white and your skirt
is black and your shirt
is white and it's
1951 again
and you're sitting
ear-pressed to the
Grundig 2066 tube
radio
toes tapping to
the Clovers
and you're
charmed by the history

bird
and there's hemlock
bourbon
and intoxicated
by this forged journey
you choose
you choose
to remain
braided in time.

60

There is a city there
just across the virus bridge
of 1893
the other side
of the Rideau River
burning
to be loved
beckoning hearts
to pump along her streets
to squeeze themselves
into her narrows
poco a poco
to trespass into
her own sinewy days
to flee Porter's Island
into the enigma
of her veil.

Even the Juggalos
restless as hummingbirds
know there will be hell
to pay

their souls too
quickened by the
trembling butterflies
of Dvořák

they make room for
breath and fury and mange
in the solitude of
Road Runner rerun afternoons

drinking Faygo
in hatchet gear
waiting for the clown
parade

waiting one soldier
at a time
one solitary stride
at a time

waiting to don petticoats
under the Philadelphia sun like
a procession of mischievous swans.

62

We move from
Cabaret of Nothingness
to Cabaret of the Inferno
to Cabaret of Sky

monks and whiskered men
and garçons of heaven
bring us spirits
in the Salle d'Intoxication

there is cholera
envy, suicide
and consumption

and by god
there is gold and
silver and song
and father time

swinging his baton
conducting an orchestra
through the great rooms of
La Belle Époque.

63

The doors of the
Surrealist Poets Gardening Association
are long closed
membership cards strewn
across the decades
like discarded skin

now
we fold coriander leaves
into tense mouths
press juniper petals
as witnesses between the pages
of darker stories

the wheelbarrows in
the botanical garden's
arid house
lounge amongst the
opuntia, haworthia and
green jade vine

there is voodoo
in the air
a volatile metaphor
at the end of each
sentence
something trapped
behind the rib cage.

64

A sky comes across
the screaming
the clocks are stuck
at an impossible time
this and every other
day stops serenading us
turns a blind eye
to our epileptic hunt
for food, hilarity
hypotheses, graphs
a room clouds into
a bastille
where the natural world
carves itself into
a bone atlas.

65

You may not tell lies
to the librarian
no dirty faces
at the reading tables
even
if you are an angel
no dogs, no food
no smallpox
no card games
no chirping, no IV bags
even
if the snowflakes
are burning.

66

The Communist Catholic
Writers Group
clubhouse
on Christie Street
sits abandoned

the poets have moved to
their private imagination prisons
some conjuring
the titian swell
of California's wild poppies

some suffering vertigo
while rubbernecking
at the red-bellied
woodpeckers
of early spring

some confabulating
with their typewriters
begging for words
to perforate
the darkness of dreaming.

67

On the 46th day
children on scooters
skateboards and
tiny atrophied feet
bushwhack
the street
como vándalo
as if it were
the holiest day
of the year
mothers and fathers
sit vigil on euphoric
verandas
reciting the second law
of thermodynamics.

68

The gendarme
asks for my walking
papers
tells me
I am insouciant
—where the fuck
did he learn *that* word—
dog and I both
stop
overhead
NORAD fire jets
perform uninvited
somersaults
my knees buckle
under the weight
of phantom bombs.

69

Curlew
curfew

a light infantry
of geese
corralling
the absence of
sound
on mud-clogged
shores.

70

Sometimes my right
ventricle speaks
to my left
says

no time for arabesque
sit
during this contorted solstice
listen to the stethoscope's
dance macabre
sit
in the gloaming
of a life well spent
sit
in wait of the sun wolf's
mouth rising
sit
as bare-chested boys do
in the empty schoolyard
feasting on
nothingness.

71

I dreamt my son was a small boy
with green fingers
and we lived in O'Clohissey's
bookshop in the by-street
and we cheated at pickup sticks
on marble floors
the colour of marigolds
and horse-faced
Buck Mulligan fed us
moss pudding
once a fortnight
and read to us
from the history
of human imagination
and we ransacked
the shelves for
cubist painters
Lost Time
Chance and
Scott's Last Expedition
before settling
on the moving waters
of the Codex Hammer.

72

Just north of here
in the gallery of regrettable foods

the lawyer is slicing pineapple
with gumption
while the doctor time-travels

soda fountain glasses
and spoons must be boiled
he reports
the 1919 weather is somewhat

caldo e umido
40 gradi
niente pioggia
cieli limpidi
turchino
azzurro
un piccolo vento

and hearts
fall
from the sky.

73

Fishing
in the flowering deserts
of Chile
amidst the ephemerals
we catch nothing
but find

yesterday, today and tomorrow
sunburnt numbers
Oppenheimer's pencil
antipoems
a small puddle
alive with soul music
a classroom
a moustache
a hotel filled
with expired sonnets
a guillotine
a semicolon
then
the smell of añañuca
and Parra's broken parrot.

81

74

Why are the girl guides
wearing their hair
like Lyle Lovett
and reading
the Scottish Witchcraft Act
instead
of collecting badges
for kissing posters
of K-pop boys
and silencing
the mouths
of fatuous
moon-bellied
bastards.

75

Today
in the post office
a day masquerading
as a great hunger
an gorta mór

today
in the grooves
of Alabama Slim's
blue and lonesome
a hush of hard times
an drochshaol

today
in estranged shop windows
silhouettes of girls
careen into
hypothetical voices
nóiméad ciúin

today
at the strand
the breakwater refuses
sinn féin
a jailbreak at the aviary
and pirate birds flood
the bowling alleys.

The dictionary lady
absquatulates

in each book
she's left
a ruffle of
the tongue
a flitter of
the lips
a tremor of
the umbra
a son
a daughter
a waltz.

77

How we see a submarine
depends

casket
spaceship
womb
bunker
body bag
temple
forest
birdhouse
wardrobe
skin
architecture
wolf belly
pi

on which chamber of the heart
we carry each other in.

78

In this light
our street becomes
a deer

the trees
billowing petticoats

the dandelions
tiny heretics

the lost coins
drops of the milky way

the chewing-gum wrappers
manifestos

the fallen leaves
librettos

the pebbles
a kinder lexicon.

79

As if
a blitzkrieg

we eat
rutabaga
Jerusalem artichoke
turnip
kohlrabi
beets
les légumes oubliés

there can be no meat
no bones
no insects
only
a new bistronomy
quiet and measured
enough
to start a revolution.

We forego
the gathering sunset
and twilight rumpus
for a nap
in hopes
of raising
the day
to the dead
of loosening and
swallowing down
the knot pleated
into the voice
into the light
of every hour
into the clavicle's
horizon
and soon
sleep steals us
into her booziness
like a warm animal
the kitchen croons
like an opium den
the city ends
its burden as
an infirmary
questions are
answered with

tenderness
the dogs are
set free
the grass begins
to grow
and no one
has to testify.

81

Some of my friends are
balcony birding
others are doing
las translations
some are burning
fingers
others burning
weeks
the tulips
don't really
give a shit
it's all punk
and pidgin
to them.

82

No panic here
today
no guns cocked
no elocution
no incoming
just a haul
of potatoes
and the soulful
click-clack
click of
the bicycle wrench.

It starts like most days
with morning coffee and the forecast
18°C
then the talk turns to clover, thistle and quack grass
the wilding of St. Stephen's Green
the 466 songs of the black-throated green warbler
the emergency and how not even
Hawkeye Pierce could save us from all this
then an epiphany
the lunch lady at R. J. Lang junior high
cafeteria trays and a deep calm unwinding
suddenly as if a fin de siècle
my brother calls announcing Slava
St. George's day
and I think maybe I should pray
but I have always been
the redder sheep of the family
I don't know the words
I begin
Caledonia soul music
$y=mx+b$
I am an island
ferry 'cross the Mersey
Leopold Bloom
my eyes are a footnote
I do not smoke cigarettes

my pyjamas are not impressed
and continue
to hold me hostage for hours
and that's okay
I realize that all these syllables
are just scars on a life lived.

84

We are a neighbourhood
without beacons
the barber poles are
still as dead deer

coiffeurs
no longer performing
tooth extractions
surgeries or haircuts

the radio towers
stuck idle under
hollow skies
mute as mercury

we turn to our own
books and blades
crank radios and
slow cooking

we send out smoke signals
chew our fingernails
loot the air as if
it was the end times

somehow we find
our own ecosystem
lodged between the
refrigerator and the sternum

it contains a Burroughs
adding machine
circa 1886
and an armistice song.

Allen Ginsberg climbs up the drainpipe, carrying a satchel full
of papers, he is Billie Holiday and Miles Davis, he is lips. He
is a singer, a Buddhist, a wavering hope, a twig snapped in half
over the back of America. *I heard, I heard, I heard,* he says, *I heard
your loneliness calling to me through the prayers of the dead. I heard your small
life crack under the weight of snowbirds, northern fauna, hospital beds and sluggish
words, I heard. I heard your fear of the supermarket whispered between joker
trees. I heard rumour of broken femurs set in papier-mâché while the daffodils
spilled over into the street for every stranger's eye, I heard. I heard the scab peeling
from your skin like rice paper and promised a promise. I heard the wind break
the cadence of your breath as if you were walking a tightrope. I heard you call the
calendar Houdini, ghost, naught, I heard. I heard the trembling of your hand
pressed against the face of a small child who was now a grown man with hair as
black as poppy seed. I heard the bodies fall like missiles and brought you wings. I
heard Georgia O'Keeffe's brush rippling over wheat and black iris, I heard her hair
as a baptism. I heard Missouri, Texas, Paris and Nelson Ball in your voice, I heard.
I heard there is something salvageable waiting for us in the beat hotel under the
eyes of Shiva. I heard the ashes of the devil in your throat, stirring up a wickedness,
I heard. I heard Burroughs and his junkie hounds howling in your backyard. I
heard the magpie conspire with the trickster spring and the knives, I heard. I heard
the portrait of Dr. Gachet taking you into its fold like the suicide sea. I heard the
orange hall and Belfast Bridges, Sandy Row crying your troubles, I heard. I heard
the sunflowers bow to the elements, then scatter like lost boys, I once heard. I heard
flags burning like stogies between the jowls of mother-fucking stooges, I heard. I
heard the bullshit, the crackling neon and the skyscrapers' wail. I heard the stitches
being ripped out, I heard the pages being torn, I heard the bending of numbers, I
heard the investigation, I heard the snake. I heard, I heard, I heard.*

We start at the end
Z Y X W
we feel like
redactionists, alchemists, seedsmen, moonlighters,
        necromancers and revisionists
greasy typesetting ink bleeders, junk haulers, volcano
        eaters, sad-eyed word benders
moving through the jeopardous molecules of heavenless days
with a hypothesis, a hidden agenda, a bloody freakishness,
        a flipside trajectory
a wild west around our necks
we tear out the letters between Dick and Jane, the beat of
        a generation
as if a resurrection, a sacrament, a trance, a lament
a cardinal, a blues riff, a yoke, a child
we thwack, thump, thud, scrub, lather and starch each letter
against the walnut-wood washboard, in a coughing house
until it glistens like a golden leaf
we hang each majuscule to swing on the clothesline
in the sunlight like a hostage
at day's end we remove the clothespins, like picking off
soldiers
we start with an A and an N and a D
we fashion a hieroglyph to be hung in the window
to remind us
there will be a tomorrow and a tomorrow
and again a tomorrow
and a name and a name
and a flutter.

The fact of
fiddleheads
at 12:43
is heroism
enough.

We are circling each other like electricity. No, a Nancy Pearl
Action Librarian figure will not cheer me up. We are sifting
through the detritus of a life so far, opening and shutting
drawers, closets, arms. Suddenly, the ice cream truck jingle
wafts through the open windows like an explosion of life,
an ornament, an oof back, all the way back to those
otherworldly days. And there is a bridge and we are
capsizing and everything could be different, but it's not.

Then we watch Shuffle in C, indigo ink-blue, blues all
the way to the bone, marrow blues. Syncopating, choking,
tearing down the house blues. Nosebleed, I miss my mama
so damn much blues. Skip James, Blind Lemon Jefferson,
Leadbelly blues. Bessie Smith, let the son into the house
blues. And the skin makes room for it and the body follows
and the bones reset themselves. And a remarkable logic
appears in the form of a flower moon.

89

I am reading Huttel, lightheartedly at first, then I'm
reminded of this war we've been in. And how he's gone and
McFadden is gone and Fred too, and it'll never be April in
my heart or ole buttermilk sky. It'll always be somewhere
down the crazy river, it'll always be translating Americans
into Canadians, floundering on the shores of Ontario lake
with a broken ukulele, willing the snarl of this fire in the
belly to flame itself out.

I am reading Huttel, hoping Arthur Rimbaud is whispering
paradise in his ear and they're eating persimmons on streets
cobbled out of stone and Buddha is not dead and Buddha is
not dead.

I tell myself, there is a joviality in this morning's brutish chinook. I am irritable and cross-eyed from want. Every day there are reports of dead poets over the newswire, and I've buried enough on my own to know what comes next.

I circle back to Dylan's rough and rowdy ways, Albuquerque moon, Boffyflow and Spike, Dextivity, but it's always and forever one flight up. And there are clouds and bare feet and eternity stones and atlases and there are natural numbers and whole numbers, whole notes, and half notes, integers and rational numbers, irrational notes, small atlases, cure atlases, G1140-G1144 atlases and secret riffs.

I wedge myself between the bebop and the blue monk, the sometimes and Sierpiński's triangle.

I will lie low today, I will sway and hum to cruelty's offbeat.

Forget the grand jury secrets
the hailstones, the street that is not my street
I've been standing on this small typo
braving the deep night
in search of the corn planting moon
like a broken chimney
I've had chaos for breakfast
lunch and dinner
watched my hair grow
into an insectarium
and yearned for the sophomoric
laugh tracks of
I Love Lucy
I've grown phantom limbs
and a wooden leg
I've baked every number
and voice you love into
midnight bread
to be eaten with apples
I've been asked
but it's hard to dance on one leg
I've been bled
of my hooliganism.

I buy a ticket to the ink-foraging party
in central park
I join a handful of "pigment enthusiasts"
we stand on Gapstow Bridge
under blimp-like umbrellas
awaiting instruction

we begin with the dangerously pink
pokeweed and move on
to pearl paint, black walnut ink
plankton
hawthorn berry
pokeberry

the man from the Toronto
ink company
speaks to us with the voice
of a chemist or poet
"petrichor" he repeats over and over
his mind is dented

in a way that makes me feel
peculiarly happy
"petrichor" I sigh
and think of
all the uninkable
things in this world.

"A crime does not occur
when white men stalk and kill
a black stranger
a crime does occur when
black people vote"
—Adam Serwer, *The Atlantic*, May 8, 2020

I am fucking around with syntax and yeast and jazz
       tuning forks refrigerators and mathematics
sonnets and saints chives and parsley and turnips
fossils and feathers and *Howl's Moving Castle*
       a crime does not occur
stats and data and pancakes, guitar strings and screamo
saffron and armchairs and Blake's dancing fairies
sound poems, beat poems, Su-primo poems
oulipo and Fermat, Tesla and middle heaven
       a crime does not occur
Little Richard, greater than and equal to
alpha, bravo, Charlie and Euclidean equations
Cyrillic soldiers, hydrogen, Marx brothers and
Dinah Washington, buckles and paradise
       a crime does not occur
blood orange and cartography, cowboys and
pencil sharpeners, the weight of paper, inertia
the philosopher's stone, a murder most foul
the manifestos, the insects the confessions
       a crime does not occur.

94

And what did you do during the great war, Mr. Joyce?

I searched for Hamlet in the leperyards and plaguegraves
with the magician of the beautiful as the oxen sun burned
the buttons off our backwards trousers, like a *yes yes yes*

I stoked the fires of Hades with the leg of a duck and took
in the scent of its bloom so much like the skin of a prayer
so much like the overturn turn over turnovers of bedlam

I Dublined the whole day pub hunting with lotus eaters
floated atop the dead sea, a giant Gaeilge lily of a man
whispering omnis caro ad te veniet, omnis caro ad te veniet

I sat in the confession box anticipating the goodness like
a moth waiting for the gloaming, a swan waiting for
his brother, like a crutch waiting for the bone to set

And what did you do?

95

There is a place that is not my home
there *is* a place that is not my home
there is

a fistful of air waiting stubbornly
on the other side of the skylight
like a blood transfusion.

96

A man takes a picture of a lake
I do not know the man, the man
is a poet, I know his words, they are
like water they are like jubilees
like the lake on fire, like the shirts
drying over the lake that is on fire
like the clothesline that flits over the lake
like a sickle so greedy for the wheat.

Sean Penn comes over for dinner, but on the lowdown. He asks me for a chicken sandwich, I eat plants. His boots are sunflower yellow from the Haitian mud although I'm not sure, it might be from the Navajo sun. He is much shorter than I imagined, I am like a transmission tower giving off morbid amounts of voltage to his 21 grams. I tell him that the first time the levees broke was when he used his fist. A live wire does not like to be touched. We are the same age, except he is three months and 23 days older than I am. He sits on my chesterfield which he calls a couch, he gives me a Harvey Keitel grin, and I know where this is going, he is no crossing guard. The dog circles like crows circling bad luck and I know it's time to let Sean back out into the wild.

We go to the Vincent van Gogh drive-in
it's like we're in a movie and a sky at the same time
and maybe a field of sunflowers
with dainty ears falling in place of stars
from the corrugated blue

we pay 38 dollars to watch the circumvolution
after-dark from the safety of our cocoons
knee to knee as if on a school excursion
thinking that maybe just maybe the rest
of this year will be more than a footnote
that maybe we'll hit it out of the park
maybe
the bandage will come off easily.

99

It is 3 a.m.
someone on my street is having a duel
I can hear it through the open window
yes, we have kept the windows open
for 40 days, quaranta giorni to let in
the heart of the city, the exhausted
parks and the lonely hair of pacifists

it's still 3 a.m. on a Saturday night and
the cafeterias are closed and the
duelists are wearing romantic
attachments in place of pants
not so dangerous, I think, then
they begin to Rumba and
Cha-cha-chá, Coro-prégon

a wisp of an intimacy
a house on fire.

I decide to join the Shakespeare and Company Lending Library
Brentano's at 27 avenue de l'Opéra on the right bank requires
far too many dictionaries, it will cost me 8 francs plus a
7-franc deposit, that makes 15

inside the bookshop I find Ezra Pound in a swimming pool
made of small egoists reading poetry maps and a wolf
disguised as the royal botanical Kew Gardens
in the corner is a woman whose name is pronounced
sylvia beach

the number on my lending card is 341 which means
I am a Canadian in Paris, guilty of nothing.

Charles Bukowski walks into an off-licence, tells the woman
with the unruly glasses he's a poet, a modern poet. Asks,
does she live on Normandy
and is her hangover as lucid as his. She looks at him like a
    trapped bird.
All she wants is her liquor, her very own hangover and to
    be left alone.

a modern poet, you say?

yes, Bukowski, you can buy my books
Bukowski, buy my books.

102

We decide to sew horses.

We collect all the needles in the house, count, 17, that'll do.
Begin with the muzzle, then chin groove, throat latch and so on
until we reach the soft place from where the heart will grow.
Each stitch must be as perfect as a breath, necessary as an
emergency. We comb the bookshelves for the fiercest verbs,
gather them as if they were embers. We suture the participles
end to end. A small amount of ink begins to flow, then a
slight rhythm.

The sun on its way to setting, the madness of our actions
sinks in and the *oh fuck* of it all leaks into the exquisite
unfolding.

Today I walked the beach and the thing I found in the sand
    that did not
look like a mouth that did not look like lightning glass that
    did not look like
a sentence that did not look like half an orange that did not
    look like a reed
that did not look like a Patti Smith song that did not look
    like a lawn chair
that did not look like a 2 or a 4 or a piece of a 7 was just the
    thing that was
just the rusty spoke of a broken year.

Before day breaks its back to leap into the light, before the
      garbage bins
begin their own demented chorus, before the robin's clipped
      confessions, before
the ending credits of the burning car dream, I hear the
      heartbreaking silence of
the recess bell, and the voice of Charles Simic saying, *go
      back to sleep, it's 3 a.m.*

June will descend from the heavens
like so many other Junes
but this June will not be like
the gargantuan parasol of
previous Junes
this June will be a crippled story
authored by a broken-fingered
poet, head full of buttons
the colour of June bugs.

106

Yesterday, on Oxford Street
a small thing happened
imperceptible as a murmur of wind
only the wind was holding its breath

a girl and a boy stepped into
a fluke of a street to watch
two ants wrestle
proof

everything is magnetic
we can never fall off the edge.

107

On today's walk

7 bicycles
1 to the beat of
Cannonball Adderley
a dizzy kind of business
4 robins setting a bird table
on the gardener's spade
1 magnolia, opus half done
38 tulips on the school's lawn
turban-clad Persian soldiers
maroon swooning 11 a.m.
$7,000^2$ x $8,000^3$ blades of grass
a gargantuan emerald
river of skin
63 minutes
countless dandelions
punctuating the run-on
sentence squatting
in my skull
and all this held and held
under one crisp blue
whole note.

108

My life walked away from me
it left a house full of buttonholes

heaps of little wound mouths
asking to be fed.

109

Coming out of sleep this morning feels like wading through
an oil spill. I make my way to the kitchen, everything looks
right, 3 lemons, the refrigerator purring gently like a sleeping
animal, a scrap of a note *wake me when the geese come*. Everything
feels right until it doesn't.

I leash the dog, marvel at his very existence, tell him I love him,
as if for the last time, and we move into the street. A confluence
of 2 shadows under an elastic sun, we feel the earth shift a
degree, click and release. Everything feels right until it doesn't.

A madness of wishing flowers, blossom after blossom
shedding their downy skirts and I don't even know what
to wish for anymore. Lawn mowers and the swishing of a
broom, a symphony on the wind, an attempted happiness.
Everything feels right until it doesn't.

David McFadden. There is always some damn poet
pacifying the chaos.I think about his trip around a life and
how it was more like a trip around a wound, and how he
filled that wound with snow and love and a white page for all
of us who would come after him.

We all have our once-around and as we walk alone and together
I hope that my once-around will be more than this simple
rhythm of circling the block, existing in the voice of others
where everything feels so right.

Newton said that gravitation is universal

why is it the dying cannot tell the living
what they really want in death?

I get a call, a man is dying, I picture the man
sitting by the lake, he loves the lake, hopes
that someday very soon, he will move
across the map of this great body of water
like a metaphor, like a fish
pulled to probability

I picture the disease as a quorum of crab
travelling at the speed of light
until they reach zero
bone, zero flesh
just the pull of the water
and the probability of metaphor.

III

It's garbage day and the bottlemen
are out hauling their blue satchels
like children with dislocated arms

they dive into bin after bin
each one an Esther Williams
or a Pythagoras holding their
breath counting 1 Mississippi
2 Mississippi, 3

while the black hole
nesting in the centre of our galaxy
grows brighter x 75
and I collect errata after errata
with which to fill
all the hollow bits.

I enrol in a hypothetical writing class taught by Steve Buscemi,
it's like diving into the deep end without arms, like standing in
a bread line during a riot, like praying underwater after
the clergy have all gone home.

Cutlery, I want you to write about cutlery and Shostakovich!
His voice is like the underbelly of a car engine, I look for the
exit sign, then remember he is my hero and my anti-hero
and maybe later he will teach us to tango.

I am erasing word after word like a third-grader, it's like
trying to write using a live wire. I am not interested in the
cutlery variable or Dmitri's Russian *Hamlet*, I want to
write a dictionary filled with all the new species of words
hatching in the ailing spring of my mind.

We are in an asymmetric war and Steve is standing at
the blackboard with his very own reference system
lips heavy as stones and eyes like a murky pond
ruminating about its guerilla-filled waters.

This morning I woke to the sound of birds whispering about the humans.

We are sorry your flags are on fire, your newspapers are inked with the blood of a son and another and another. We hear the cracking of bones all the way down 12th Street, when you think no one is looking. We have seen tear gas flower over city after city while you huddled in doorways like broken teeth. We hear the creak of war's door opening while some fly kites and others kiss the feet of Jesus. We feel the earth tearing out her hair, shifting position, filling her lungs with the last breaths of innocent men and women. We hear her weeping into the flames and over the rubber bullets dropping into the boulevard like chestnuts. We know what the black and the blue and the electrifying night bring and we know what it means to be dying to live. We know the names by heart: Birmingham, Philadelphia, Watts, Flint, Baltimore, Los Angeles, Twin Cities, and sometimes when you are asleep, we recite them back to you in hopes that the hate growing inside your children might spiral out of them like a final breath.

Acknowledgements

During the most terrifying seventy-eight days of my life, I sat at my dining room table in Toronto and knocked off poem after poem. What else was I supposed to do during the spring 2020 pandemic lockdown? I began posting the poems on Facebook; soon, the encouragement and support tempered the dread I was feeling and gave me hope.

I am endlessly grateful to all those first readers, especially my gracious and very talented friend Gary Barwin, who suggested that these daily dispatches might become a book.

A special thank-you to my friend and exceptional writer Stuart Ross, who oversaw this book and brought it to press. You have such great instincts and passion, and I am so fortunate to have you as an editor.

Thank you also to:
Jim Smith and Nicholas Power for their unwavering support and friendship.

Drew, Aria, and Miles for putting up with my shenanigans and without whom I couldn't do any of this.

Lastly, to my dog Ozzy, who walked the neighbourhood with me every one of those seventy-eight days.

Lillian Nećakov is the author of six books of poetry and numerous chapbooks, broadsides, and leaflets. Her book *The Lake Contains an Emergency Room* was shortlisted for the 2016 bpNichol Chapbook Award. During the 1980s she ran a micropress called The Surrealist Poets Gardening Assoc. and sold her books on Toronto's Yonge Street.

Lillian was on the selection committee for Toronto's fourth and fifth Poet Laureates and was an advisory board member for the third Poet Laureate's Poetry Is Public and Poetry Legacy Project. She ran the Boneshaker Reading series from 2010 to 2020.

She lives in Toronto and just might be working on a new book.

Other Feed Dog Books from Anvil Press

"A Feed Dog Book" is an imprint of Anvil Press edited by Stuart Ross and dedicated to contemporary poetry under the influence of surrealism. We are particularly interested in seeing such manuscripts from members of diverse and marginalized communities. Write Stuart at razovsky@gmail.com.

The Least You Can Do Is Be Magnificent: New & Selected Writings of Steve Venright, compiled and with an afterword by Alessandro Porco (2017)
I Heard Something, by Jaime Forsythe (2018)
On the Count of None, by Allison Chisholm (2018)
The Inflatable Life, by Mark Laba (2019)
Float and Scurry, by Heather Birrell (2019)
The Headless Man, by Peter Dubé (2020)
Queen and Carcass, by Anna van Valkenburg (2020)

an imprint of Anvil Press